BE PART OF THE TEAM!

ON THE SOCCER TEAM

STEPHANE HILLARD

PowerKiDS press

New York

Published in 2022 by The Rosen Publishing Group, Inc.
29 East 21st Street, New York, NY 10010

First Edition

Portions of this work were originally authored by Mason Burdick and published as *Soccer*. All new material in this edition was authored by Stephane Hillard.

Editor: Greg Roza
Book Design: Michael Flynn

Photo Credits: Cover (soccer player), p. 19 SDI Productions/E+/Getty Images; cover, pp. 10, 14, 16, 18, 20 (soccer ball) pikepicture/iStock/Getty Images; p. 4 The Good Brigade/DigitalVision/Getty Images; p. 5 Anita van Zyl/Gallo Images/Getty Images; p. 7 Topical Press Agency/Hulton Archive/Getty Images; p. 9 David Madison/Stone/Getty Images; p. 11 Erik Isakson/Blend Images/Getty Images; p. 13 Grady Reese/Corbis/VCG/Getty Images; p. 15 leolintang/Shutterstock.com; p. 17 Kris Timken/Getty Images; p. 21 AGIF/Shutterstock.com.

Library of Congress Cataloging-in-Publication Data

Names: Hillard, Stephane, author.
Title: On the soccer team / Stephane Hillard.
Description: New York : PowerKids Press, [2022] | Series: Be part of the
  team! | Includes index.
Identifiers: LCCN 2020037845 | ISBN 9781725327757 (library binding) | ISBN
  9781725327733 (paperback) | ISBN 9781725327740 (6 pack)
Subjects: LCSH: Soccer–Juvenile literature.
Classification: LCC GV943.25 .H57 2022 | DDC 796.334–dc23
LC record available at https://lccn.loc.gov/2020037845

Manufactured in the United States of America

CPSIA Compliance Information: Batch #CSPK22. For Further Information contact Rosen Publishing, New York, New York at 1-800-237-9932.

Find us on

CONTENTS

TEAMWORK!

Soccer is a sport that requires teamwork. Teammates pass a ball back and forth to keep it away from the other team. They score points by kicking the ball into a goal. They do it all without using their hands!

Soccer is one of the most popular team sports in the world. That might be because it doesn't take much to start a game— just a soccer ball and a group of friends. You can even practice your soccer skills by yourself.

Soccer players learn to use their feet, knees, chest, and head to control the ball and score goals.

SOCCER THROUGH THE YEARS

Games similar to soccer have been played since ancient times. The sport we're familiar with today took shape in England in 1863. That year, the first official rules were recorded.

Soccer's popularity in the United States has had its ups and downs. Other sports, such as baseball and football, have been more popular. However, kids and teens play for school and town **leagues** across the country. **Professional** soccer in the United States is growing in popularity as more fans are drawn to the sport.

Two English teams play a game of soccer (called "football" in many countries) in 1913.

TEAM TALK

Soccer may not be the most popular sport in the United States, but it is by far the most popular sport in the world. Studies show there are 3.5 billion soccer fans around the world!

FIELD FACTS

A soccer field is 100 yards (91 m) long and 60 yards (55 m) wide. At each end is a goal that is 24 feet (7.3 m) wide and 8 feet (2.4 m) tall.

At the center of the field is a circle. Players on **offense** start there with the ball at the beginning of the game and after the other team scores a goal. The **defense** must stay out of this circle until the offense touches the ball.

TEAM TALK

The large rectangle in front of each goal is called the **penalty** area. Breaking a rule inside the penalty area can give the other team a chance to score up close.

GOAL

GOAL AREA ▷

◁ **PENALTY AREA** ▷

◁ **SIDELINE** ▷

◁ **SIDELINE**

CENTER CIRCLE ▷

END LINE

GOAL

The smaller rectangle inside the penalty area is the goal area. When the offense misses the goal, the goalie places the ball on a corner of this box and kicks it to a teammate.

9

PLAYER POSITIONS

Soccer teams have 11 players on the field. Goalies stand in front of their own nets. They can touch the ball with their hands if they are inside the penalty area.

Defenders play closest to their goalie and try to stop the other team from scoring. Next come midfielders. They have to be fast because they switch between offense and defense often. Forwards play the farthest away from their own goalie. They're usually the best scorers on the team.

No matter what **position** they play, all players on a soccer team are expected to help out on both offense and defense.

ON ATTACK

The offense controls the ball and keeps it away from the defense. Players try to kick the ball into the other team's goal to score a point. Teammates work together to get this done.

Offense often starts when the goalie throws or kicks the ball down the field. Players on offense get control of the ball and attack the other team's goal. Offensive players pass the ball to each other to set up plays while keeping it away from defensive players.

TEAM TALK

If a defensive player kicks the ball over the end line near their own goalie, the offense gets a free kick from the corner of the field. Corner kicks can result in exciting goals.

Moving the ball up the field to get a goal takes patience, skill, and lots of teamwork.

SOLID DEFENSE

It's the job of the defense to stop the offense from scoring. They run after the offensive players and try to take the ball from them. They can do this by **intercepting** a pass.

Defenders must be good at tackling. Soccer players don't pull other players to the ground when tackling. Instead, they use their feet to take the ball away from the offense. During a slide tackle, the defender slides in front of another player and takes the ball away.

A well-trained defense can take the ball away from the offense using an **offside** trap. Defenses do this by rushing forward as the offense is trying to get by them.

Slide tackles can be very exciting, but also very dangerous. Players have to be careful not to hit the other player, which would result in a penalty.

The goalie guards their team's goal. This can be hard because the goal is so big! Goalies use their hands to catch the ball or punch it away from the goal. Once they have the ball, goalies can roll, throw, or kick it to teammates.

The goalie is the last line of defense. Goalies must be quick and strong to stop a running forward who's about to score. Once they have the ball, goalies shout directions to their teammates and set up plays.

Goalies may need to make diving saves! Because of this, they often wear long pants and shirts. They also wear thick gloves.

DON'T BREAK THE RULES!

Breaking a rule gives the other team an **advantage**. A team might get a free kick. This gives the kicking team time to set up a play and score. Penalties inside the penalty area can result in free kicks very close to the goal.

Soccer officials use colored cards to announce penalties. A yellow card is a warning. A player who gets a red card must leave the game. Getting two yellow cards is the same as getting a red card.

Most soccer games have a main official called a referee, and two assistant referees. Sideline judges are also needed to let referees know when the ball goes out of bounds.

IN THE PROS

People of all ages all over the world love playing soccer. Some play it on a grass field. Some play it on a dirt lot. Some even play in a parking lot or in the streets. Beach soccer is also popular.

Many countries, including the United States, have professional leagues. The best players get to play for their country once every 4 years in the World Cup. Winning the FIFA World Cup Trophy is a great honor, but it takes teamwork!

SOCCER TALK

ASSIST	TO PASS THE BALL TO A TEAMMATE, WHO THEN SCORES.
CROSS	A KICK THAT SENDS THE BALL FROM NEAR A SIDELINE ACROSS THE FIELD AND IN FRONT OF THE GOAL.
FIFA	SHORT FOR FÉDÉRATION INTERNATIONALE DE FOOTBALL ASSOCIATION, THE INTERNATIONAL GOVERNING BODY FOR THE SPORT OF SOCCER.
PENALTY KICK	A FREE SHOT TAKEN FROM 12 YARDS (11 M) IN FRONT OF THE GOAL, USUALLY AS A RESULT OF A PENALTY THAT HAPPENS INSIDE THE PENALTY AREA.
STOPPER	A TALENTED DEFENDER WHO IS GOOD AT STOPPING FORWARDS.
STRIKER	A TALENTED FORWARD PLAYER AND GOOD SCORER.
SWEEPER	A DEFENDER WHO PLAYS BEHIND THE OTHER DEFENDERS AND GOES WHERE THEY ARE MOST NEEDED.
THROW-IN	TO THROW THE BALL BACK INTO PLAY WHEN THE OTHER TEAM KICKS IT PAST A SIDELINE. THIS IS THE ONLY TIME A PLAYER OTHER THAN THE GOALIE CAN TOUCH THE BALL WITH THEIR HANDS.

GLOSSARY

advantage: The fact of being in a better condition than others.

defense: The act of trying to stop the other team from scoring.

intercept: To take a pass meant for a player on the other team.

league: A group of sports teams that play each other one or more times during a season.

offense: The act of trying to score points.

offside: When a player on offense is between the last defender and the goal when a pass is made to that player.

penalty: A loss one team or player must take for breaking a rule.

position: The role a person plays on a sports team. Also, the location on the field where those players commonly play.

professional: Having to do with something done for money and not just for fun.

FOR MORE INFORMATION

BOOKS

Kingsly, Imogen. *Soccer Fun*. North Mankato, MN: Capstone Press, 2021.

Scheff, Matt. *The World Cup: Soccer's Greatest Tournament*. Minneapolis, MN: Lerner Publications, 2020.

WEBSITES

Basic Soccer Rules
www.kids-play-soccer.com/basic-soccer-rules.html
Visit this website to learn more about the rules of soccer.

Major League Soccer
www.mlssoccer.com/
MLS is the U.S. men's professional soccer league.

INDEX